T0159213

The Kingman Comprehension Series

Intermediate Level 5

Dr. Alice Kingman

PARTRIDGE

ISBN: Softcover   978-1-5437-7384-2
            eBook   978-1-5437-7385-9

To order additional copies of this book, contact
Toll Free +65 3165 7531 (Singapore)
Toll Free +60 3 3099 4412 (Malaysia)
orders.singapore@partridgepublishing.com

www.partridgepublishing.com/singapore

Contents

Acknowledgements

First, I would like to thank Jazzy, the illustrator of the Kingman Comprehension Series, for her beautiful artistic drawings which bring every story she has worked on to life.

My great appreciation is also to be extended to my two daughters, Stephanie and Audrey, who helped me from the very beginning in the typing and formatting of questions for every reading passage.

A big thank you to my beloved husband, Matt, for his continuous support, encouragement and professional assistance in the computerised structuring of the book.

I am also grateful to all my students for their contributions to this project, working on different passages, testing out questions and providing invaluable feedback.

With no reservation, my heartfelt gratitude goes to my beloved late father, Joseph, who spared no effort in teaching me English since I was seven years old.

Thank you to all other members of my family who spurred me on to take this big step in realising my dreams of becoming an English-language author. I thank them for their love and patience throughout the whole process. Thank you to my wonderful church family as well for their uplifting prayers and support.

Last but not least, I thank God, my Heavenly Father, every day for His unfailing presence and spiritual guidance, without which this project would not have happened.

To Teacher and Parent

In my lifelong career as an English-language teacher, I have often been disappointed and discouraged to find questions set for comprehension passages stressing speedy location of answers or meticulous reproduction of the text. The formulated questions seldom encourage students to read between the lines or genuinely understand the writer's choice of diction and intention of writing. In other words, students are often deprived of opportunities to think out of the box and explore implied meanings and examine the purpose of sentence structure.

Hence, it has always been my ambition to produce a comprehension series that can sharpen students' skills in analytical discernment. The Kingman Comprehension Series comprises high-interest selections of different literary genres from classics to renowned children's literature including fables, folk and fairy tales, poems, legends, myths as well as modern realistic fictions. It is my hope that students will find the works of the outstanding authors in the books not only enjoyable to work on but also interesting enough to spark further independent reading among themselves.

The Dragons of Blueland

Ruth Stiles Gannett

It wasn't until the next morning that the "dragon affair" came out in the "Nevergreen City News."

"Listen to this!" yelled Mr. Elevator, reading aloud at breakfast: "'A fantastic and unexplainable escape took place in the great, high mountains of Blueland late Sunday night. Fifteen dragons, a wonder in themselves as they have long been believed extinct …'" and the newspaper story went on to tell about the brave men who had fought their way back through treacherous sandstorms to tell "the most momentous story of our time."

"'Unbelievers who doubt this story,'" continued Mr. Elevator, reading aloud from the paper, "'will find it difficult to dismiss the following supporting evidence of the presence of dragons in this region.'" Then he proceeded to read about a ship stationed off the coast of Popsicornia which twice had sighted a strange flying beast, once with a boy atop it. And about a certain Mr. Wagonwheel who claimed also to have seen it twice, once on the ground near his farm, and once in the air with a boy aboard, over Seaweed City. And about Chester DeWitt, a small boy who also claimed he'd seen the dragon over the city the preceding Thursday evening. Lastly, there was a short bit about the conductor and the ticket agent, who wondered if the boy they had seen late Sunday night could have had anything to do with the case, and so on.

Mr. Elevator dropped the paper and stared at Elmer. "Did you have anything to do with all this? I just don't understand your strange trips away from home."

"Me?" said Elmer, choking on a piece of toast. "Why, Father, you don't mean you really believe all that nonsense, do you?"

Answer the following questions.

1. The *Nevergreen City News* is most probably the _____ of the town.

2. The escape of the 15 dragons was not described as
   a. funny   b. remarkable   c. inexplicable

3. What two factors made the story the most momentous story of the time?

4. Use the word "dismiss" in the correct part of speech in the following sentences:
   a. The administrators _____ the suggestions John made yesterday.
   b. The _____ of the taxi driver who spoke to her very rudely was abrupt.

5. Why would one tend to believe what Mr. Wagonwheel said about what he saw?

6. Match the following character with the correct descriptions:

   a. was not an old man.

   b. claimed he'd seen the dragon over the city.

   Chester DeWitt   c. claimed he'd seen the dragon the previous Tuesday.

   d. also claimed he'd seen the dragon twice.

   e. claimed he'd fought with the dragon.

7. The conductor and the ticket agent, who were colleagues, probably worked at
   a. a railway station   b. the airport   c. a bicycle rental shop

8. Change the following question to indirect speech.
   "Did you have anything to do with all this?" Mr. Elevator asked Elmer.
   Mr. Elevator asked Elmer if _____
   _____.

9. What made Mr. Elevator suspect Elmer's being involved in the whole incident?

10. How did Elmer react when Mr. Elevator questioned him about his involvement?

11. What would be a striking headline for this article in the *Nevergreen City News*?

12. Would you like to read the full text of this story? Why or why not?

Read on:

In this children's fantasy novel, Boris the baby dragon returns to his homeland in the high mountains of Blueland, only to find that his big dragon family is in danger, being trapped in a cave by men. His only hope is to fly to Nevergreen City to ask Elmer, the young friend who has saved him from Wild Island, to rescue his folks.

Unlike the first book, *My Father's Dragon*, the illustrations within the book are black and white lithographs, done again by the author's stepmother, Ruth Chrisman Gannett.

Ching Yuh And Kyain Oo. The Trials Of Two Heavenly Lovers

A Korean Story

Translated by Horace Newton Allen

The examination was held in a great enclosure at the rear of the palace, where the King and his counsellors sat in a pavilion upon a raised stage of masonry. The hundreds of men and youths from all parts of the country were seated upon the ground under large umbrellas. Pang Noo was given a subject and soon finished his essay, after which he folded it up carefully and tossed the manuscript over a wall into an enclosure, where it was received and delivered to the board of examiners. These gentlemen, as well as His Majesty, were at once struck with the rare merit of production and made instant inquiry concerning the writer. Of course, he was successful, and a herald soon announced that Pang, the son of You Tah Jung, had taken the highest honours. He was summoned before the King, who was pleased with the young man's brightness and wisdom. In addition to his own rank, his father was made governor of a province and made haste to come to court and thank his sovereign for the double honour and to congratulate his son.

Pang was given permission to go and bow at the tomb of his ancestors, in grateful acknowledgement for Heaven's blessings. He went to pay his respects to his mother, who fairly worshipped her son now, if she had not <u>done so</u> before. During his absence, the King had authorised the board of appointments to give him the high rank of *Ussa*, for though he was young, His Majesty thought one so wise and quick well fitted to travel in disguise and spy out the acts of evil officials, learn the condition of the people, and bring the corrupt and usurious to punishment. Pang Noo was amazed at his success, yet the position just suited him, for aside from a desire to better the condition of his fellow men, he felt that in this position, he would be apt to learn the whereabouts of his lady-love, whose beautiful vision was ever before him. Donning a suitable disguise, therefore, he set out upon the business at hand with a light heart.

Answer the following questions.

1. Where was the examination held?

2. Give two reasons why the King and his counsellors were seated on a raised platform.

3. What did Pang Noo have to do on finishing his essay?

4. _____ _____ _____ _____, as well as _____ _____, examined the manuscript written by Pang Noo.

5. Which part of the sentence in the first paragraph shows the examiners were all impressed by Pang Noo's essay?

6. True or False:
   a. A herald announced that You Tah Jung had taken the highest honours. _____
   b. The King was pleased with Pang Noo's brightness and fairness. _____
   c. Only Pang Noo was given a rank in the kingdom. _____

7. In the second paragraph, the words "done so" in the sentence "if she had not done so before" implies Pang Noo's mother had been _____ _____ _____ for some time.

8. Why did the King promote Pang Noo to a high rank though he was young?

9. Would the evil officials recognise that a high-rank officer was coming to spy on them? Why or why not?

10. Which was not a mission of Pang Noo's travel?
    a. to learn the condition of the people
    b. to execute the evil officials
    c. to have those who were corrupted apprehended

11. Which part of the sentence in the second paragraph suggests that even Pang Noo was astonished at what he had achieved?

12. What would really please Pang Noo besides bettering people's living conditions?

Read on:

Found in *Korean Tales*, translated from the Korean folklore by Horace Newton Allen, the story of 'Ching Yuh And Kyain Oo' follows the scholastic success of Pang Noo and his pursuit of his lady-love. The country, the people, the government and the culture of Korea are colourfully described. Horace Newton Allen was a missionary, physician and American ambassador to Korea, arriving there in 1884. Other stories in the book are 'The Rabbit and Other Legends' and 'The Enchanted Wine Jug.'

Bed in Summer

Robert Louis Stevenson

In winter I get up at night

And dress by yellow candle-light.

In summer, quite the other way,

I have to go to bed by day.

I have to go to bed and see

The birds still hopping on the tree,

Or hear the grown-up people's feet

Still going past me in the street.

And does it not seem hard to you,

When all the sky is clear and blue,

And I should like so much to play,

To have to go to bed by day?

Answer the following questions.

1. In this poem, each stanza has four lines, which is called a couplet / a tercet / a quatrain.

2. The rhyme scheme employed in this poem is _____/_____/_____.

3. Between the first and second verses, enjambment (a striding over) is used to
    a. carry the reader smoothly to the next line
    b. create a sense of delay
    c. create a sense of suspense

4. Why is the yellow candle-light needed when the poet gets up in winter?

5. Why does the poet go to bed by day in summer?

6. What can the poet see and hear when he goes to bed in summer?

7. True or False:
    a. The poet likes to go to bed early in summer. _____
    b. The poet is a bit jealous of the birds and adults. _____

8. The verse "When all the sky is clear and blue" is an example of the imagery of seeing / hearing / smelling / tasting / touching.

9. Give two pieces of evidence to show why we believe the poet is a child.

10. The poet addresses the readers in the last stanza by asking a question. This poetic technique is called
    a. personification   b. a metaphor   c. apostrophe

11. The message of this poem is that
    a. the poet really dislikes winter
    b. the poet's daily routine changes depending on the season
    c. the poet enjoys activities outside his house

12. Do you like this poem? Why or why not?

Read on:

'Bed in Summer', a short children's poem written by Robert Louis Stevenson, tells of a young child who feels saddened by the knowledge that he misses out much because of the effects of the changing seasons on sleeping habits.

This poem, with its visual delights, appears to be very innocent and appeals a lot to children.

The Princess Mayblossom

Madame d'Aulnoy

They had hardly begun to get the Princess ready when a dwarf arrived, mounted upon an elephant. He came from the five fairies, and brought for the Princess a crown, a sceptre, and a robe of golden brocade, with a petticoat marvellously embroidered with butterflies' wings. They also sent a casket of jewels, so splendid that no one had ever seen anything like it before, and the Queen was perfectly dazzled when she opened it. But the Princess scarcely gave a glance to any of these treasures, for she thought of nothing but Fanfaronade. The Dwarf was rewarded with a gold piece, and decorated with so many ribbons that it was hardly possible to see him at all. The Princess sent to each of the fairies a new spinning-wheel with a distaff of cedar wood, and the Queen said she must look through her treasures and find something very charming to send <u>them</u> also.

When the Princess was arrayed in all the gorgeous things the Dwarf had brought, she was more beautiful than ever, and as she walked along the streets the people cried: 'How pretty she is! How pretty she is!'

The procession consisted of the Queen, the Princess, five dozen other princesses her cousins, and ten dozen who came from the neighbouring kingdoms; and as they proceeded at a stately pace the sky began to grow dark, then suddenly the thunder growled, and rain and hail fell in torrents. The Queen put her royal mantle over her head, and all the princesses did the same with their trains. Mayblossom was just about to follow their example when a terrific croaking, as of an immense army of crows, rooks, ravens, screech-owls, and all birds of ill-omen was heard, and at the same instant a huge owl skimmed up to the Princess, and threw over her scarf woven of spiders' webs and embroidered with bats' wings. And then peals of mocking laughter rang through the air, and they guessed that this was another of the Fairy Carabosse's unpleasant jokes.

The Queen was terrified at such an evil omen, and tried to pull the black scarf from the Princess's shoulders, but it really seemed as if it must be nailed on, it clung so closely.

'Ah!' cried the Queen, 'can nothing appease this enemy of ours? What good was it that I sent her more than fifty pounds of sweetmeats, and as much again of the best sugar, not to mention two Westphalia hams? She is as angry as ever.'

Answer the following questions.

1. The dwarf didn't bring for the Princess
    a. a crown   b. a robe   c. butterflies' wings

2. Give evidence to show that the casket of jewels was very special.

3. Which of the following could have "dazzled" your eyes?
    a. a bronze statue   b. an iron lock   c. a diamond necklace

4. Why did the Princess hardly look at the treasures?

5. The two words "scarcely" and "hardly" are
    a. synonyms   b. antonyms   c. homonyms

6. The pronoun "them" in the last line of the first paragraph is referring to _____ _____.

7. Which four words in the second paragraph describe what the Princess was wearing?

8. What three phenomena changed the weather condition of the day?

9. What did the Queen and all the princesses cover their heads with?

10. What two sounds could be heard from all the birds of bad luck?

11. Why couldn't the Queen remove the black scarf from the Princess's shoulders?

12. How much sugar did the Queen give to Fairy Carabosse?

Read on:
'The Princess Mayblossom,' a French literary fairy tale by Madame d'Aulnoy in 1697, is about a much-wanted child, a princess, who is cursed by Fairy Carabosse to be miserable for her first 20 years of life. When her 20th birthday nearly comes, Princess Mayblossom falls in love with the ambassador who is supposed to make an offer for a prince to wed the princess. In the end, the ambassador proves to be unworthy of Princess Mayblosom's love, but the prince does.

Gulliver's Travels

Part 1, Chapter 1

Jonathan Swift

What became of my companions in the boat, as well as those who escaped on the rock or were left in the vessel, I cannot tell but conclude they were all lost. For my own part, I swam as fortune directed me and was pushed forward by wind and tide.

I often let my legs drop and could feel no bottom, but when I was almost gone and able to struggle no longer, I found myself within my depth, and, by this time, the storm was much abated. The declivity was so small that I walked near a mile before I got to the shore, which I conjectured was about eight o'clock in the evening.

I then advanced forward near half a mile but could not discover any sign of houses or inhabitants; at least, I was in so weak a condition that I did not observe them. I was extremely tired, and with that and the heat of the weather and about half a pint of brandy that I drank as I left the ship, I found myself much inclined to sleep. I lay down on the grass, which was very short and soft, where I slept sounder than ever I remembered to have done in my life, and as I reckoned, about nine hours; for when I awaked, it was just daylight. I attempted to rise but was not able to stir, for as I happened to lie on my back, I found my arms and legs were strongly fastened on each side to the ground; and my hair, which was long and thick, tied down in the same manner. I likewise felt several slender ligatures across my body, from my armpits to my thighs. I could only look upwards, the sun began to grow hot, and the light <u>offended</u> my eyes. I heard a confused noise about me, but in the posture I lay, could see nothing except the sky.

In a little time, I felt something alive moving on my left leg, which, advancing gently forward over my breast, came almost up to my chin; when bending my eyes downward, as much as I could, I perceived it to be a human creature, not six inches high, with a bow and arrow in his hands and a quiver at his back. In the meantime, I felt at least 40 more of the same kind (as I conjectured) following the first. I was in the utmost astonishment and roared so loud that they all ran back in a fright, and some of them, as I was afterwards told, were hurt with the falls they got by leaping from my sides upon the ground.

However, they soon returned, and one of them, who ventured so far as to get a full sight of my face, lifting up his hands and eyes by way of admiration, cried out in a shrill but distinct voice—"Hekinah degul!" the others repeated the same words several times, but I then knew not what they meant.

Answer the following questions.

1. It is believed that only the writer of the story _____ in the accident at sea.

2. Which factor was not one that helped the writer to get ashore?
   a. the wind   b. the storm   c. the tide   d. good fortune

3. Fill in the blanks with the correct words: abated / conjectured / attempted
   a. I _____ he would come to the party late as he was so busy.
   b. Though the storm _____, a lot of damage had been caused.
   c. Grandpa _____ to fix the tail lights of the car but failed this morning.

4. Were there inhabitants on the island? Underline the part of the sentence in the third paragraph that supports your answer.

5. Why was the writer much inclined to fall asleep on reaching the shore?

6. Which part of the sentence suggests the writer was dead to the world for a while?

7. True or False:
   a. The writer was not able to move much on waking up. _____
   b. The writer could move his hands and legs freely. _____

8. "The light offended my eye" is an example of a simile / a metaphor / personification.

9. Why was it that the writer could see nothing except the sky?

10. What indicates that the little human creature came armed?

11. "Hekinah degul" is an example of a beautiful / native / simple language.

12. Arrange the following sentences in the correct sequence:
    _____ The writer felt something moving over his body.
    _____ The writer tried to move.
    _____ The writer arrived on the island.
    _____ The writer was tied down.

Read on:

When the boat Lemuel Gulliver is travelling on is hit and destroyed in a storm, the protagonist swims for his life and is stranded on the island of Lilliput. Upon waking up, Gulliver finds himself being tied up by the Lilliputians, who happen to be very small people. *Gulliver's Travels* is a story involving several adventurous voyages. After each one, Gulliver returns to his home in England, where he recovers from the incredible experiences and then sets out again on a new expedition.

Rebecca of Sunnybrook Farm

Kate Douglas WigginJean Webster

When Rebecca alighted from the train at Maplewood and hurried to the post office where the stage was standing, what was her joy to see uncle Jerry Cobb holding the horses' heads.

"The reg'lar driver's sick," he explained, "and when they sent for me, thinks I to myself, my drivin' days is over, but Rebecky won't let the grass grow under her feet when she gits her aunt Jane's letter, and like as not I'll <u>ketch</u> her to-day; or if she <u>gits</u> delayed, to-morrow for certain. So here I be jest as I was more 'n six years ago. Will you be a real lady passenger, or will ye sit up in front with me?"

Emotions of various sorts were all struggling together in the old man's face, and the two or three bystanders were astounded when they saw the handsome, stately girl fling herself on Mr. Cobb's dusty shoulder <u>crying like a child</u>. "Oh, uncle Jerry!" she sobbed; "dear uncle Jerry! It's all so long ago, and so much has happened, and we've grown so old, and so much is going to happen that I'm fairly frightened."

"There, there, lovey," the old man whispered comfortingly, "we'll be all alone on the stage, and we'll talk things over 's we go along the road an' mebbe they won't look so bad."

Every mile of the way was as familiar to Rebecca as to uncle Jerry; every watering-trough, grindstone, red barn, weather-vane, duck-pond, and sandy brook. And all the time she was looking backward to the day, seemingly so long ago, when she sat on the box seat for the first time, her legs dangling in the air, too short to reach the footboard. She could smell the big bouquet of lilacs, see the pink-flounced parasol, feel the stiffness of the starched buff calico and the hated prick of the black and yellow porcupine quills. The drive was taken almost in silence, but it was a sweet, comforting silence both to uncle Jerry and the girl.

Then came the sight of Abijah Flagg shelling beans in the barn and then the Perkins attic windows with a white cloth fluttering from them. She could spell Emma Jane's loving thought and welcome in that little waving flag; a word and a message sent to her just at the first moment when Riverboro chimneys rose into view . . .

Answer the following questions.

1. Rebecca got off the train at _____ and stopped at _____ _____ _____ .

2. Underline the idiom (eight words in the second paragraph) that means "won't hesitate to get something done."

3. In the second paragraph, the words "ketch" should be spelled _____ and "gits" should be spelled _____ .

4. A real lady, according to uncle Jerry Cobb, will sit _____ the driver.
    a. in front of   b. with   c. behind

5. Change the following question into indirect speech.
    "Will you be a real lady passenger or will ye sit up in front with me?"
    Uncle Jerry Cobb asked Rebecca if_____
    _____ .

6. How did the two or three bystanders feel when they saw Rebecca crying like a child on Mr. Cobb's shoulder?

7. The expression "crying like a child" in the third paragraph is an example of
    a. a simile   b. a metaphor   c. personification

8. True or False:
    a. Rebecca and uncle Jerry knew the way well. _____
    b. The scenery along the way was barren and boring. _____

9. How do we know Rebecca was just a little girl when she sat on the box seat for the first time?

10. What could Rebecca smell, see, and feel along the way?

11. Uncle Jerry and Rebecca enjoyed the fact that they weren't talking much. Why?

12. The little white flag flying at the Perkins attic window says
    a. "Have a good day!"   b. "Be safe and happy!"   c. "Welcome home!"

Read on:
Eleven-year-old Rebecca Randall, an impulsive and carefree child, is leaving her beloved Sunnybrook Farm to live with her two stern but well-to-do aunts and get an education. The story follows the girl's growth and maturing into a young lady who charms everyone she comes across.

Wizard of Oz

L. Frank Baum

When Dorothy was left alone, she began to feel hungry, so she went to the cupboard and cut herself some bread, which she spread with butter. She gave some to Toto, and taking a pail from the shelf, she carried it down to the little brook and filled it with clear, sparkling water. Toto ran over to the trees and began to bark at the birds sitting there. Dorothy went to get him, and saw such delicious fruit hanging from the branches that she gathered some of it, finding it just what she wanted to help out her breakfast.

Then she went back to the house, and having helped herself and Toto to a good drink of the cool, clear water, she set about making ready for the journey to the City of Emeralds.

Dorothy had only one other dress, but that happened to be clean and was hanging on a peg beside her bed. It was gingham, with checks of white and blue; and although the blue was somewhat faded with many washings, it was still a pretty frock. The girl washed herself carefully, dressed herself in the clean gingham, and tied her pink sunbonnet on her head. She took a little basket and filled it with bread from the cupboard, laying a white cloth over the top. Then she looked down at her feet and noticed how old and worn her shoes were.

"They surely will never do for a long journey, Toto," she said.

And Toto looked up into her face with his little black eyes and wagged his tail to show he knew what she meant.

At that moment, Dorothy saw lying on the table the silver shoes that had belonged to the Witch of the East.

"I wonder if they will fit me," she said to Toto. "They would be just the thing to take a long walk in, for they could not wear out."

She took off her old leather shoes and tried on the silver ones, which fitted her as well as if they had been made for her.

Finally, she picked up her basket.

"Come along, Toto," she said. "We will go to the Emerald City and ask the Great Oz how to get back to Kansas again."

Answer the following questions.

1. Dorothy cut herself some bread because she was _____.

2. Did Dorothy eat the bread plain? How do you know?

3. What kind of animal was Toto? Give evidence.

4. Dorothy picked some delicious fruit hanging from the branches. Why?

5. In the second paragraph, the expression "helped herself and Toto to" means
    a. consumed   b. spilled   c. give away   d. wasted

6. Match the dress Dorothy had beside her bed with the correct descriptions:

    Dorothy's dress
    a. was hanging on a peg.
    b. had on it checks of black and white.
    c. had somehow faded in colour with many washings.
    d. was washed by Dorothy herself.
    e. came with a sunbonnet tied to it.

7. Why did Dorothy lay a white cloth over the top of the basket?

8. What didn't go well with the pretty frock Dorothy was wearing?

9. How did Toto show he understood what Dorothy meant about her shoes?

10. If there were a Witch of the East, there might be a Witch of the _____.

11. Did the silver shoes fit Dorothy well? How do you know?

12. Arrange the following sentences in the correct sequence:
    _____ Dorothy ate bread with Toto.
    _____ Dorothy put on her clean dress.
    _____ Dorothy tried on the silver shoes.
    _____ Dorothy and Toto headed for Emerald City.

Read on:

When a tornado hits Kansas, Dorothy and her dog, Toto, are swept up and plonked down in the land of Oz, a magical kingdom. On the way, Dorothy encounters three friends: the Scarecrow, the Tin Man and the Cowardly Lion. Together, they embark on a quest to see Wizard, who is believed to be able to help her return home and grant the others' wishes. Over a century after its publication, *Wizard of Oz* remains one of the best-known stories in American literature, declared by the Library of Congress to be "America's greatest and best-loved homegrown fairy tale."

The Voyages of Doctor Dolittle

Hugh Lofting

My name was Tommy Stubbins, son of Jacob Stubbins, the cobbler of Puddleby-on-the-March, and I was nine and a half years old. At that time, Puddleby was only quite a small town. A river ran through the middle of it, and over this river, there was a very old stone bridge, called Kingsbridge, which led you from the market-place on one side to the churchyard on the other.

Sailing ships came up on this river from the sea and anchored near the bridge. I used to go down and watch the sailors unloading the ships upon the river-wall. The sailors sang strange songs as they pulled upon the ropes, and I learned these songs by heart. And I would sit on the river-wall with my feet dangling over the water and sing with the men, pretending to myself I too was a sailor.

For I longed always to sail away with those brave ships when they turned their backs on Puddleby Church and went creeping down the river again, across the wide lonely marshes to the sea. I longed to go with them out into the world to seek my fortune in foreign lands—Africa, India, China, and Peru! When they got round the bend in the river and the water was hidden from view, you could still see their huge brown sails towering over the roofs of the town, moving onward slowly—like some gentle giants that walked amongst the houses without noise. What strange things would they have seen, I wondered, when next they came back to anchor at Kingsbridge! And dreaming of the lands I had never seen, I'd sit on there, watching till they were out of sight.

Three great friends I had in Puddleby in those days. One was Joe, the mussel man, who lived in a tiny hut by the edge of the water under the bridge. This old man was simply marvellous at making things. I never saw a man so clever with his hands. He used to mend my toy ships for me, which I sailed upon the river; he built windmills out of packing-cases and barrel-staves; and he could make the most wonderful kites from old umbrellas.

Joe would sometimes take me in his mussel boat, and when the tide was running out, we would paddle down the river as far as the edge of the sea to get mussels and lobsters to sell. And out there on the cold lonely marshes, we would see wild geese flying and curlews and redshanks and many other kinds of seabirds that live amongst the samfire and the long grass of the great salt fen. And as we crept up the river in the evening, when the tide had turned, we would see the lights on the Kingsbridge twinkle in the dusk, reminding us of tea-time and warm fires.

Another friend I had was Matthew Mugg, the cat's-mean-man. He was a funny old person with a bad squint. He looked rather awful, but he was really quite nice to talk to. He knew everybody in Puddleby, and he knew all the dogs and all the cats.

Answer the following questions.

1. One side of Kingbridge was the _____-_____ and the other side, the _____.

2. What did the sailors do when they were unloading upon the river-wall?

3. Underline the phrase (two words in the second paragraph) that suggests the writer remembered the songs well.

4. True or False:
   a. The writer wanted to seek his fortune in Africa, India, China and Japan. _____
   b. The writer had been daydreaming about lands he had never seen before. _____

5. What was the last thing that could still be seen of the ships as they sailed away?

6. What were the ships compared to?

7. Underline the two sentences in the fourth paragraph that tell us the writer admired the things his friend, Joe, made.

8. What two things didn't Joe make?
   a. toy ships
   b. windmills
   c. kites
   d. umbrellas

9. In your own words, tell when the writer and Joe usually returned.

10. Which of the two seafoods Doctor Dolittle and Joe sold would fetch more money?

11. The phrase "with a squint" tells us Matthew Mugg could not
   a. sing too well   b. see too well   c. smell too well   d. hear too well

12. Would you like to be able to talk to animals? Why or why not?

Read on:

The book *The Story of Doctor Dolittle*, written and illustrated by Hugh Lofting, is the first of the series of Doctor Dolittle books.

The physician in the story prefers animal patients, with which he can communicate in their own languages. Doctor Dolittle finally gives up entirely being a doctor for humans, whom he shuns, and becomes a naturist who dedicates the rest of his life to learn more about animals and nature.

May Flowers

Louisa May Alcott

Being Boston girls, of course they got up a club for mental improvement, and, as they were all descendants of the Pilgrim Fathers, they called it the Mayflower Club. A very good name, and the six young girls who were members of it made a very pretty posy when they met together, once a week, to sew, and read well-chosen books. At the first meeting of the season, after being separated all summer, there was a good deal of gossip to be attended to before the question, "What shall we read?" came up for serious discussion.

Anna Winslow, as president, began by proposing, "Happy Dodd;" but a chorus of "I've read it!" made her turn to her list for another title.

"'Prisoners of Poverty' is all about workingwomen, very true and very sad; but Mamma said it might do us good to know something of the hard times other girls have," said Anna, soberly; for she was a thoughtful creature, very anxious to do her duty in all ways.

"I'd rather not know about sad things, since I can't help to make them any better," answered Ella Carver, softly patting the apple blossoms she was embroidering on a bit of blue satin.

"But we might help if we really tried, I suppose; you know how much Happy Dodd did when she once began, and she was only a poor little girl without half the means of doing good which we have," said Anna, glad to discuss the matter, for she had a little plan in her head and wanted to prepare a way for proposing it.

"Yes, I'm always saying that I have more than my share of fun and comfort and pretty things, and that I ought and will share them with some one. But I don't do it; and now and then, when I hear about real poverty, or dreadful sickness, I feel so wicked it quite upsets me. If I knew HOW to begin, I really would. But dirty little children don't come in my way, nor tipsy women to be reformed, nor nice lame girls to sing and pray with, as it all happens in books," cried Marion Warren, with such a remorseful expression on her merry round face that her mates laughed with one accord.

Answer the following questions.

1. Which part of the United States were the Boston girls from?
   a. the north
   b. the south
   c. the east
   d. the west

2. The girls called their club the _____ _____ because their ancestors were the _____ _____.

3. Name two activities the girls were engaged in when they met once a week.

4. Why was there always a lot of talking amongst the girls about other people before any serious discussions?

5. Which two words between the first and third paragraphs tell us that more than one girl has read the book *Happy Dodd*?

6. Give one reason why Anna suggested reading *Prisoners of Poverty*.

7. Use two adjectives to describe Anna. Explain.

8. What was Ella doing while listening to the others' ideas?

9. Was Anna ready to drop the idea of trying to help the poor? Why or why not?

10. The kind of life Marion had not been leading
    a. funful
    b. comfortable
    c. wicked
    d. privileged

11. What were Marion's two main reasons for not sharing with the needy?

12. Underline the phrase (three words in the last paragraph) that means "in a unified way."

Read on:

In the story of 'May Flowers' by Louisa May Alcott, also the author of *Little Women*, a group of six young Boston girls, growing up in Victorian times, call themselves the May Flowers as they are all descendants of the Pilgrims.

They form a small club and meet once a week to sew and read well-chosen books for mental improvement and expansion of horizons. Through the sessions, the girls discover the power of kindness and the privilege of sharing abundance.

The Chameleon

Anton Chekhov

THE police superintendent Otchumyelov is walking across the market square wearing a new overcoat and carrying a parcel under his arm. A red-haired policeman strides after him with a sieve full of confiscated gooseberries in his hands. There is silence all around. Not a soul in the square. . . . The open doors of the shops and taverns look out upon God's world disconsolately, like hungry mouths; there is not even a beggar near them.

"So you bite, you damned brute?" Otchumyelov hears suddenly. "Lads, don't let him go! Biting is prohibited nowadays! Hold him! ah . . . ah!"

There is the sound of a dog yelping. Otchumyelov looks in the direction of the sound and sees a dog, hopping on three legs and looking about her, run out of Pitchugin's timber-yard. A man in a starched cotton shirt, with his waistcoat unbuttoned, is chasing her. He runs after her, and throwing his body forward falls down and seizes the dog by her hind legs. Once more there is a yelping and a shout of "Don't let go!" Sleepy countenances are protruded from the shops, and soon a crowd, <u>which</u> seems to have sprung out of the earth, is gathered round the timber-yard.

"It looks like a row, your honour . . ." says the policeman.

Otchumyelov makes a half turn to the left and strides towards the crowd.

He sees the aforementioned man in the unbuttoned waistcoat standing close by the gate of the timber-yard, holding his right hand in the air and displaying a bleeding finger to the crowd. On his half-drunken face there is plainly written: "I'll pay you out, you rogue!" and indeed the very finger has the look of a flag of victory. In this man Otchumyelov recognises Hryukin, the goldsmith. The culprit who has caused the sensation, a white borzoy puppy with a sharp muzzle and a yellow patch on her back, is sitting on the ground with her fore-paws outstretched in the middle of the crowd, trembling all over. There is an expression of misery and terror in her tearful eyes.

"What's it all about?" Otchumyelov inquires, pushing his way through the crowd. "What are you here for? Why are you waving your finger . . . ? Who was it shouted?"

Answer the following questions.

1. Where is the police superintendent when the story begins? Is he alone? Explain.

2. Which two sentences suggest the square is empty?

3. The confiscated gooseberries in the hands of the red-haired policeman have probably been taken from
   a. the orchard   b. the kitchen   c. the grocery   d. a hawker

4. The open doors of the shops and taverns are compared to _____ _____.

5. What is the new law issued in the city?

6. Why is the dog hopping on three legs?

7. Has the man succeeded in catching the dog? How so?

8. The relative pronoun "which" in the third paragraph is referring to
   a. the sleepy countenances   b. the shop   c. the crowd

9. The policeman says, "It looks like a row, Your Honour . . ."
   The "row" in this context is a line of people/an argument, and "Your Honour" is referring to _____.

10. Underline the phrase (four words in the sixth paragraph) that suggests the man in an unbuttoned waistcoat is injured.

11. Match Hryukin with the correct descriptions:

	a. is a goldsmith.
	b. is trembling all over.
Hyrukin	c. has his finger sprained.
	d. has a look of victory on his face.
	e. is half drunk.

12. The name of the police superintendent, Otchumyelov, suggests that the setting of this story is in England / Canada / Russia.

Read on:

In the story 'The Chameleon,' Russian writer Anton Chekhov expresses the truth about the flippant nature of human behaviour induced by different situations and settings as exhibited by a police officer. Various themes on authority, identity status and corruption are delved into, and the criterion for judging based on a genuine kindness of justice is clearly questioned.

The Prince and the Pauper

Mark Twain

Tom Canty, left alone in the prince's cabinet, made good use of his opportunity. He turned himself this way and that before the great mirror, admiring his finery, then walked away, imitating the prince's high-bred carriage and still observing results in the glass. Next, he drew the beautiful sword and bowed, kissing the blade and laying it across his breast, as he had seen a noble knight do, by way of salute to the lieutenant of the Tower, five or six weeks before, when delivering the great lords of Norfolk and Surrey into his hands for captivity. Tom played with the jewelled dagger that hung upon his thigh; he examined the costly and exquisite ornaments of the room; he tried each of the sumptuous chairs and thought how proud he would be if the Offal Court herd could only peep in and see him in his grandeur. He wondered if they would believe the marvellous tale he should tell when he got home or if they would shake their heads and say his overtaxed imagination had at last upset his reason.

At the end of half an hour, it suddenly occurred to him that the prince was gone a long time; then right away, he began to feel lonely; very soon he fell to listening and longing and ceased to toy with the pretty things about him; he grew uneasy, then restless, then distressed.

Suppose someone should come and catch him in the prince's clothes and the prince not there to explain. Might they not hang him at once and inquire into his case afterward? He had heard that the great were prompt about small matters. His fears rose higher and higher, and trembling, he softly opened the door to the antechamber, resolved to fly and seek the prince, and through him, protection and release. Six gorgeous gentlemen-servants and two young pages of high degree, clothed like butterflies, sprung to their feet and bowed low before him. He stepped quickly back and shut the door. He said,

"Oh, they mock at me! They will go and tell. Oh! Why came I here to cast away my life?"

He walked up and down the floor, filled with nameless fears, listening, starting at every trifling sound. Presently, the door swung open, and a silken page said,

"The Lady Jane Grey."

Answer the following questions.

1. Where did Tom Canty find himself left all alone?

2. Tom Canty looked at himself in the mirror and acted as if he were a _____ _____.

3. Who were captured five to six weeks ago?
   a. the prince
   b. the lieutenant of the Tower
   c. the lord of Norfolk
   d. the lord of Surrey

4. Which word suggests the dagger was one beautifully set with gems?

5. In your own words, say what Tom Canty was worried about that his friends would say when he told them the story of becoming a prince.

6. How did Tom Canty feel when he realised the prince had been gone for long?

7. What did Tom Canty fear would happen to him immediately on being found a "fake" prince?

8. Name the part of speech of the two underlined words.
   a. to "toy": _____   b. his fears "rose": _____

9. What did Tom Canty want to seek through the prince?

10. The gentlemen-servants and pages outside were compared to _____.

11. Was Tom Canty clear about what he was frightened about? Support your answer with a phrase (three words between the third and sixth paragraphs).

12. Put the following sentences in the correct sequence:
    _____ Tom Canty toyed with the ornaments in the chamber.
    _____ Lady Jane Grey entered the chamber.
    _____ Tom Canty imagined how his friends would react.
    _____ Tom Canty was fearful for his life.

Read on:
Written by American author, Mark Twain, and published in 1881, *The Prince and the Pauper* is a novel belonging to the genre of realistic fiction.
Set in 1547, the story tells of how a chance encounter gives two young boys, who were born on the same day and identical in appearance, an opportunity to experience a way they have always envied. Tom Canty is a pauper who lives in abject poverty but freely, and Prince Edward is the son of Henry VIII of England.

The Conceited Apple Branch

Hans Christian Andersen

Danish Nordic Scandinavian

There came now across the fields a whole group of children, the youngest of <u>whom</u> was so small that he had to be carried by the others; and when he was seated on the grass, amongst the yellow flowers, he laughed aloud with joy, kicked out his little legs, rolled about, and plucked the yellow flowers and kissed them in childlike innocence.

The older children broke off the flowers with long stems, bent the stalks one round the other to form links, and made first a chain for the neck, then one to go across the shoulders and hang down to the waist, and at last a wreath to wear about the head; so that they looked quite <u>splendid</u> in the rings of green stems and golden flowers. But the oldest amongst them gathered carefully the faded flowers, on the stem of which were grouped together the seeds, in the form of a white feathery crown.

These loose, airy wool flowers are very beautiful and look like fine snowy feathers or down. The children held them to their mouths and tried to blow away the whole crown with one puff of breath. They had been told by their grandmothers that whoever did so would be sure to have new clothes before the end of the year. The hated flower was raised to the positive of a predicator of events.

"Do you see," said the sunbeam, "do you see the beauty of these flowers? Do you see their powers of giving pleasure?"

"Yes, to children," said the apple bough.

As time went on, an old woman came into the field and, with a blunt knife without a handle, began to dig round the roots of some of the dandelion plants and pull them up. With some, she planned to make tea for herself, but the rest she was going to see to the chemist and earn money.

"But beauty is of higher value than all this," said the apple-tree branch; "only the chosen ones can be admitted into the worlds of the beautiful. There is a difference between plants, just as there is a difference between men."

Then the sunbeam spoke of the boundless love of God as seen in creation and over all that lives, and of the equal distribution of His gifts, both in time and in eternity.

"That is your opinion," said the apple bough.

Answer the following questions.

1. The relative pronoun "whom" in the first line of the passage is referring to _____ _____
_____ _____ _____.

2. How do we readers know that the youngest child was very small?

3. Underline the five verbs used to describe the actions of the child.

4. Which phrase (three words in the first paragraph) means "not acting like an adult"?

5. How did the children wear the chains of flowers?

6. An antonym for the word "splendid" in the second paragraph is
   a. marvellous   b. unimpressive   c. magnificent

7. What were the grouped seeds of the faded flowers compared to?

8. In what way was the hated flower a predicator of events?

9. What tool did the old woman use to dig up round the roots of the dandelion plants?

10. What would the woman do with the dandelion plants?

11. True or False:
    According to the apple-tree bough, all the men are the same. _____
    Find evidence to support your answer.

12. Did the apple-bough agree to what the sunbeam said? How do you know?

Read on:

In the story 'The Conceited Apple Branch,' Hans Christian Andersen describes a fresh and beautiful but snobby apple blossom branch that looks down on the plain and unattractive presentation of the dandelion flowers, very much like some proud humans who despise or pity those who are, in their own minds, inferior to them.

Then comes a young countess who teaches the apple branch the accurate meaning of true beauty and the honourable principle of humanity.

Mr. Nobody

Anonymous

I know a funny little man,
　　As quiet as a mouse,
Who does the <u>mischief</u> that is done
　　In everybody's house!
There's no one ever sees his face,
　　And yet we all agree
That every plate we break was cracked
　　By Mr. Nobody.

'Tis he who always tears out books,
　　Who leaves the door ajar,
He pulls the buttons from our shirts,
　　And scatters pins afar;
That squeaking door will always squeak,
　　For prithee, don't you see,
We leave the oiling to be done
　　By Mr. Nobody.

He puts damp wood upon the fire
　　that kettles cannot boil;
His are the feet that bring in mud,
　　And all the carpets soil.
The papers always are mislaid;
　　Who had them last, but he?
There's no one tosses them about
　　But Mr. Nobody.

The finger marks upon the door
　　By none of us are made;
We never leave the blinds unclosed,
　　To let the curtains fade.
The ink we never spill; the boots
　　That lying round you see
Are not our boots,—they all belong
　　To Mr. Nobody.

25

Answer the following questions.

1. Do we know who the poet of the poem "Mr. Nobody" is? Why or why not?

2. In the first stanza, Mr. Nobody is described as a _____ _____ man who is as _____ as _____ _____, which is an example of
    a. a simile   b. a metaphor   c. enjambment

3. Look up in your dictionary the meaning of the word "mischief." Fill in the blank with the correct form of the word.
    "Have you ever seen a little boy as _____ as Tom?" asked the teacher.

4. True or False:
    a. Mr. Nobody is found in only some people's houses. _____
    b. The plates that are broken are cracked first. _____

5. Which of the following is not what Mr. Nobody is blamed for?
    a. The books being torn.
    b. The door being left open.
    c. The pins being scattered.
    d. The badges being pulled from shirts.

6. The door is described to be making a sound like a _____. It is an example of a poetic device called
    a. alliteration   b. onomatopoeia   c. contrast

7. What is wrong with putting damp wood upon the fire?

8. When something is mislaid, we can/cannot locate it easily. Give three other words beginning with the prefix "mis."

9. The verse "By none of us are made" (inversion) will be better understood if written "Are made by none of us." Why is this poetic device used in the poem?

10. What causes the curtains to fade?

11. Would you like to have a Mr. Nobody in your house? Why or why not?

12. Could the title of this poem be changed to 'Mr. Anybody'? Explain.

Read on:

The little man in the poem 'Mr. Nobody' is a quiet but mischievous character blamed for every mishap that occurs in everyone's house. The poem seems to feature family life where nobody, children mainly, wants to live up to the blunder or mess one creates. Anaphora, caesura, and imagery are employed to bring the fun of this poem to life.

The Sword in the Stone

T. H. White

"Excuse me, sir," said the Wart, "but can you tell me the way to Sir Ector's castle, if you don't mind?"

The aged gentleman put down his bucket and looked at him. "Your name would be the Wart."

"Yes, sir, please, sir."

"My name," said the old man, "is Merlyn."

"How do you do?"

"How do."

When these formalities had been concluded, the Wart had leisure to look at him more closely. The magician was staring at him with a kind of unwinking and benevolent curiosity, which made him feel it would not be at all rude to stare back, no ruder than it would be to stare at one of his guardian's cows, who happened to be thinking about his personality as she leaned her head over a gate.

Merlyn had a long white beard and long white moustaches, which hung down on either side of it. Close inspection showed he was far from clean. It was not that he had dirty fingernails or anything like that, but some large bird seemed to have been nesting in his hair. The Wart was familiar with the nests of Spar-hark and Gos, the crazy conglomerations of sticks and oddments, which had been taken over from squirrels or crows, and he knew how the twigs and the tree foot were splashed with white mutes, old bones, muddy feathers, and castings. This was the impression he got from Merlyn. The old man was streaked with droppings over his shoulders, amongst the stars and triangles of his gown, and a large spider was slowly lowering itself from the tip of his hat as he gazed and slowly blinked at the little boy in front of him. He had a worried expression, as though he were trying to remember some name that began with Choi but was pronounced in quite a different way, possibly Menzies, or was it Dalziel? His mild blue eyes, very big and round under the tarantula spectacles, gradually filmed and clouded over as he gazed at the boy, and then he turned his head away with a resigned expression as though it was all too much for him after all.

"Do you like peaches?"

"Very much indeed," said the Wart, and his mouth began to water so that it was full of sweet, soft liquid.

"They are scarcely in season," said the old man reprovingly, and he walked off in the direction of the cottage.

Answer the following questions.

1. The little boy, the Wart, did not know how to go to _____ _____ _____.

2. Was the Wart a well-mannered character? Give two reasons for your answer.

3. The exchange of pleasantries conducted between the Wart and the magician are part of a discussion / an examination / an interview / formalities.

4. What gave the Wart the courage to stare back at the magician?

5. Who/What is "she" underlined in the seventh paragraph referring to?

6. Which would probably have disturbed the Wart the least regarding the magician's appearance?
   a. He had dirty fingernails.
   b. He had birds nesting in his hair.
   c. He was streaked with droppings over his shoulders.
   d. A large spider was lowering itself from his hat.

7. Describe the magician's gown and spectacles.

8. Could the magician eventually see the Wart clearly? How do you know?

9. Change to indirect speech. "Do you like peaches?"
   The magician asked the Wart _____.

10. Do you think the Wart liked peaches? Explain your answer.

11. Arrange the following sentences in the correct sequence:
    _____ The magician put down his bucket to look at the Wart.
    _____ The magician walked off not terribly interested.
    _____ The magician had a worried expression on his face.
    _____ The magician studied the Wart closely.

12. *The Sword in the Stone* is considered an example of
    a. an epic   b. a tragedy   c. a legend   d. science fiction

Read on:

The Sword in the Stone, written by T. H. White in 1938, follows the story of an orphan boy named the Wart, who later becomes the legendary King Arthur of England by pulling a sword from a stone. After encountering Merlyn, an old man and magician in the woods, the Wart remains enchanted, wide-eyed and receptive throughout his tutorials with the wizard.

The Enchanted Castle

Edith Nesbit

"There *is* no other end," said Gerald with firm triumph. "It's a clue—that's what it is. What price cold mutton now? I've always felt something magic would happen someday, and now it has."

"I expect the gardener put it there," said Jimmy.

"With a Princess's silver thimble on it? Look! There's a crown on the thimble."

There was.

"Come," said Gerald in low urgent tones, "if you are adventurers, *be* adventurers, and anyhow, I expect someone has gone along the road and bagged the mutton hours ago."

He walked forward, winding the red thread round his fingers as he went. And it was a clue, and it led them right into the middle of the maze. And in the very middle of the maze, they came upon <u>the wonder</u>.

The red clue led them up two stone steps to a round grass plot. There was a sundial in the middle, and all round against the yew hedge, a low, wide marble seat. The red clue ran straight across the grass and by the sundial and ended in a small brown hand with jewelled rings on every finger. The hand was, naturally, attached to an arm, and that had many bracelets on it, sparkling with red and blue and green stones. The arm wore a sleeve of pink and gold brocaded silk, faded a little here and there but still extremely imposing, and the sleeve was part of a dress, which was worn by a lady who lay on the stone seat asleep in the sun. The rosy gold dress fell open over an embroidered petticoat of a soft green colour. There was old yellow lace the colour of scalded cream, and a thin white veil spangled with silver stars covered the face.

"It's the enchanted Princess," said Gerald, now really impressed. "I told you so."

"It's the Sleeping Beauty," said Kathleen. "It is—look how old-fashioned her clothes are, like the pictures of Marie Antoinette's ladies in the history book. She has slept for a hundred years. Oh, Gerald, you're the eldest, you must be the Prince, and we never knew it."

Answer the following questions.

1. Gerald felt very proud of himself that he knew exactly what was going on—he felt he made his discovery with _____ _____.

2. What did Gerald feel all along would happen?

3. What was found on the Princess's silver thimble?

4. When Gerald said, "If you are adventurers, *be* adventurers", the verb "*be*" in italics is to stress
    a. the urgency to be courageous
    b. the need to dress up like warriors
    c. the hesitancy to go on adventures

5. The conjunction "and" has been used three times in the sixth paragraph. It is an example of a literary device called
    a. asyndeton   b. polyptoton   c. polysyndeton

6. Where did the red clue end?

7. Which two words in the seventh paragraph suggest the arm of the Princess was grand and impressive in appearance?

8. How many colours could be detected in the magical garden? What are they?

9. What made Kathleen think of Sleeping Beauty when she saw the enchanted Princess lying there on the bench?

10. Kathleen was also reminded of _____ _____ _____ in the _____ book.

11. Which part of the sentence in the last paragraph suggests Kathleen never thought of Gerald being the Prince?

12. After reading the passage, can you guess what the wonder in the sixth paragraph is referring to?

Read on:

The Enchanted Castle, a children's fantasy novel by Edith Nesbit, tells the story of three children, who, while playing in the forest, discover a secret passageway into the garden of an old castle. There, they make-believe that the place is enchanted, and on a bench, a princess who has slept for a hundred years lies.

Little Women

Louisa Mae Alcott

"Give them all my dear love and a kiss. Tell them I think of them by day, pray for them by night, and find my best comfort in their affection at all times. A year seems very long to wait before I see them, but remind them that while we wait we may all work, so that these hard days need not be wasted. I know they will remember all I said to them, that they will be loving children to you, will do their duty faithfully, fight their bosom enemies bravely, and conquer themselves so beautifully, that when I come back to them I may be fonder and prouder than ever of my little women."

Everybody sniffed when they came to that part; Jo wasn't ashamed of the great tear that dropped off the end of her nose, and Amy never minded the rumpling of her curls as she hid her face on her mother's shoulder and sobbed out, "I am a selfish girl! but I'll truly try to be better, so he mayn't be disappointed in me by and by."

"We all will!" cried Meg. "I think too much of my looks, and hate to work, but won't any more, if I can help it."

"I'll try and be what he loves to call me, 'a little woman,' and not be rough and wild; but do my duty here instead of wanting to be somewhere else," said Jo, thinking that keeping her temper at home was a much harder task than facing a rebel or two down South.

Beth said nothing, but wiped away her tears with the blue army-sock, and began to knit with all her might, losing no time in doing the duty that lay nearest her, while she resolved in her quiet little soul to be all that father hoped to find her when the year brought round the happy coming home.

Mrs. March broke the silence that followed Jo's words, by saying in her cheery voice, "Do you remember how you used to play Pilgrim's Progress when you were little things? Nothing delighted you more than to have me tie my piece-bags on your backs for burdens, give you hats and sticks and rolls of paper, and let you travel through the house from the cellar, which was the City of Destruction, up, up, to the house-top, where you had all the lovely things you could collect to make a Celestial City."

"What fun it was, especially going by the lions, fighting Apollyon, and passing through the Valley where the hobgoblins were!" said Jo.

"I liked the place where the bundles fell off and tumbled downstairs," said Meg.

"I don't remember much about it, except that I was afraid of the cellar and the dark entry, and always liked the cake and milk we had up at the top. If I wasn't too old for such things, I'd rather like to play it over again," said Amy, who began to talk of renouncing childish things at the mature age of twelve.

Answer the following questions.

1. Mr. March would be away for _____ year, and he found great comfort in the _____ of his daughters.

2. What was Mr. March's advice to his daughters?

3. Match the daughters of the Marches with the correct statements:

	a. will be loving children to their mother.
	b. will do their duty well.
The March girls	c. will make their father proud.
	d. are called their father's little women.

4. Which word in the second paragraph suggests that the girls were a bit emotional?

5. Change the following sentence into indirect speech:
   "I think too much of my looks, and hate to work, but won't anymore, if I can help it," cried Meg.
   Meg cried that she _____
   _____.

6. What should Jo do and not do to deserve to be called "a little woman"?

7. Who was the quietest person in the family? Why do you think so?

8. How many females were there in the family? Who were they?

9. The expression "broke the silence" means
   a. ended a period of quiet
   b. pierced the atmosphere with a scream
   c. shattered the relationship

10. True or False:
    a. The children played games of imagination when they were young. _____
    b. The Celestial City was made in the basement of the house. _____

11. What did Amy like and dislike most about the imaginary play?

12. Underline the part of the sentence that implies Amy was a precocious girl.

Read on:

Written by Louisa May Alcott, *Little Women* is a coming-of-age novel that follows the lives of four sisters—Meg, Jo, Beth, and Amy. Guided by their mother and their strong religious faith, the four girls grow up in New England and discover the meaning of life and love. Each faces her own personal problems and moral challenges bravely and honestly, and eventually find her place in the world.

Black Beauty

Anna Sewell

At this time, I used to stand in the stable, and my coat was brushed every day 'til it shone like a rook's wing. It was early in May, when there came a man from Squire Gordon's, who took me away to the Hall. My master said, "Goodbye, Darkie, be a good horse, and always do your best." I could not say "goodbye," so I put my nose into his hand. He patted me kindly, and I left my first home. As I lived some years with Squire Gordon, I may as well tell something about the place.

Squire Gordon's Park skirted the village of Birtwick. It was entered by a large iron gate, at which stood the first lodge, and then you trotted along on a smooth road between clumps of large old trees, then another lodge and another gate, which brought you to the house and the gardens. Beyond this lay the home paddock, the old orchard, and the stables. There was accommodation for many horses and carriages, but I need only describe the stable into which I was taken; this was very roomy, with four good stalls; a large swinging window opened into the yard, which made it pleasant and airy.

The first stall was a large square one, shut in behind with a wooden gate; the others were common stalls, good stalls but not nearly so large. It had a low rack for hay and a low manger for corn; it was called a loose box because the horse that was put into it was not tied up but left loose to do as he liked. It is a great thing to have a loose box.

Into this fine box the groom put me. It was clean, sweet, and airy. I never was in a better box than that, and the sides were not so high but that I could see all that went on through the iron rails that were at the top.

He gave me some very nice oats, he patted me, spoke kindly, and then went away.

When I had eaten my corn, I looked round. In the stall next to mine stood a little fat grey pony with a thick mane and tail, a very pretty head, and a pert little nose.

I put my head up to the iron rails at the top of my box and said, "How do you do? What is your name?"

He turned round as far as his halter would allow, held up his head, and said, "My name is Merrylegs. I am very handsome, I carry the young ladies on my back, and sometimes I take our mistress out in the low chair. They think a great deal of me, and so does James. Are you going to live next door to me in the box?"

I said, "Yes."

Answer the following questions.

1. The coat of the horse was compared to _____ _____ _____. This literary technique is called
   a. a simile   b. inversion   c. alliteration   d. a metaphor

2. What did the horse do because it could not say goodbye? Why couldn't he say goodbye?

3. Was Squire Gordon's Park in the centre or on the outside of the village of Birtwick? Quote one word to support your answer.

4. True or False:
   a. One had to go past two gates before reaching the house and the gardens. _____
   b. Black Beauty was interested in describing all the stables he saw there. _____

5. What made the stall pleasant and airy?

6. What is the pronoun "It" in the second line of the third paragraph referring to?

7. In addition to being clean, sweet and airy, name four other privileges of being in the first stall.

8. "Into this fine box the groom put me" is an example of a literary device called
   a. enjambment   b. inversion   c. alliteration

9. Give two examples to show that the groom treated the horse kindly.

10. What details indicate that the little fat grey pony was a handsome pony?

11. Merrylegs carries on its back
    a. children   b. helpers   c. mistresses   d. masters

12. "So does James" means _____.

Read on:

Black Beauty, written by English novelist Anna Sewell and published in 1877, is set in England in the 19th century. Black Beauty, a well-born and well-bred horse, narrates the story. Initially trained and owned by caring, responsible homes, Black Beauty is sold to crueller owners under whom he suffers overwork, ill treatment and neglect.

Sewell died in 1878, and *Black Beauty* remains her only novel. Nonetheless, the author's good intention of arousing society's awareness to the plight of exploited horses and her plea for a more animal-caring attitude makes her book a classic children's fiction.

The Peterkin Papers

Lucretia P. Hale

This was Mrs. Peterkin. It was a mistake. She had poured out a delicious cup of coffee, and, just as she was helping herself to cream, she found she had put in salt instead of sugar! It tasted bad. What should she do? Of course she couldn't drink the coffee; so she called in the family, for she was sitting at a late breakfast all alone. The family came in; they all tasted, and looked, and wondered what should be done, and all sat down to think.

At last Agamemnon, who had been to college, said, "Why don't we go over and ask the advice of the chemist?" (For the chemist lived over the way, and was a very wise man.)

Mrs. Peterkin said, "Yes," and Mr. Peterkin said, "Very well," and all the children said they would go too. So the little boys put on their india-rubber boots, and over they went.

Now the chemist was just trying to find out something which should turn everything it touched into gold; and he had a large glass bottle into which he put all kinds of gold and silver, and many other valuable things, and melted them all up over the fire, till he had almost found what he wanted. He could turn things into almost gold. But just now he had used up all the gold that he had round the house, and gold was high. He had used up his wife's gold thimble and his great-grandfather's gold-bowed spectacles; and he had melted up the gold head of his great-great-grandfather's cane; and, just as the Peterkin family came in, he was down on his knees before his wife, asking her to let him have her wedding-ring to melt up with all the rest, because this time he knew he should succeed, and should be able to turn everything into gold; and then she could have a new wedding-ring of diamonds, all set in emeralds and rubies and topazes, and all the furniture could be turned into the finest of gold.

Now his wife was just consenting when the Peterkin family burst in. You can imagine how mad the chemist was! He came near throwing his crucible—that was the name of his melting-pot—at their heads. But he didn't. He listened as calmly as he could to the story of how Mrs. Peterkin had put salt in her coffee.

At first he said he couldn't do anything about it; but when Agamemnon said they would pay in gold if he would only go, he packed up his bottles in a leather case, and went back with them all.

First he looked at the coffee, and then stirred it. Then he put in a little chlorate of potassium, and the family tried it all round; but it tasted no better. Then he stirred in a little bichlorate of magnesia. But Mrs. Peterkin didn't like that. Then he added some tartaric acid and some hypersulphate of lime. But no; it was no better. "I have it!" exclaimed the chemist,—"a little ammonia is just the thing!"

No, it wasn't the thing at all.

Answer the following questions.

1. Mrs. Peterkin made a mistake. She put _____ into her cup of coffee.

2. How do we know Agamemnon was well educated?

3. What did Agamemnon suggest doing?
   Agamemnon suggested they _____.

4. Arrange the following sentences in the correct sequence:
   _____ The little boys joined their parents to go ask advice of the chemist.
   _____ Mrs. Peterkin put salt into her coffee.
   _____ The Peterkins entered the house of the chemist.
   _____ Mrs. Peterkin was ready to put cream into the coffee.

5. What was the chemist experimenting on at the moment?

6. Was it expensive for the chemist to buy gold? How do you know?

7. Which two items had not been used by the chemist in his experiment?
   a. the gold thimble of his aunt
   b. the gold-bowed spectacles of his great-grandfather
   c. the gold head of his great-great-grandfather's cane
   d. the wedding-ring of his wife

8. Which word in the fifth paragraph suggests that the chemist's wife would agree to the request?

9. Was the chemist pleased with the Peterkins' visit? What makes you think so?

10. What made the chemist change his mind about being able to do something about the salted coffee?

11. Whom was the author addressing when she wrote, "No, it wasn't the thing at all"?

12. As a reader, what would you suggest doing to make the coffee drinkable again?

Read on:

Originally published in 1880, 'The Lady Who Put Salt in Her Coffee' is the first story in *The Peterkin Papers*, a collection of humorous short stories by American author Lucretia Peabody Hale. When Mrs. Peterkin is ready to add cream to her coffee, she realises she has put in salt instead of sugar. The entire family then embarks on a remarkable quest to find someone, a chemist and a herb woman, to undo her mistake yet to no avail.

Alice's Adventures in Wonderland

Lewis Carroll

Down the Rabbit-Hole

Alice was beginning to get very tired of sitting by her sister on the bank, and of having nothing to do: once or twice she had peeped into the book her sister was reading, but it had no pictures or conversations in it, 'and what is the use of a book,' thought Alice 'without pictures or conversation?'

So she was considering in her own mind (as well as she could, for the hot day made her feel very sleepy and stupid), whether the pleasure of making a daisy-chain would be worth the trouble of getting up and picking the daisies, when suddenly a White Rabbit with pink eyes ran close by her.

There was nothing so *very* remarkable in that; nor did Alice think it so *very* much out of the way to hear the Rabbit say to itself, 'Oh dear! Oh dear! I shall be late!' (when she thought it over afterwards, it occurred to her that she ought to have wondered at this, but at the time it all seemed quite natural); but when the Rabbit actually *took a watch out of its waistcoat-pocket*, and looked at it, and then hurried on, Alice started to her feet, for it flashed across her mind that she had never before seen a rabbit with either a waistcoat-pocket, or a watch to take out of it, and burning with curiosity, she ran across the field after it, and fortunately was just in time to see it pop down a large rabbit-hole under the hedge.

White Rabbit checking watch

In another moment down went Alice after it, never once considering how in the world she was to get out again.

The rabbit-hole went straight on like a tunnel for some way, and then dipped suddenly down, so suddenly that Alice had not a moment to think about stopping herself before she found herself falling down a very deep well.

Either the well was very deep, or she fell very slowly, for she had plenty of time as she went down to look about her and to wonder what was going to happen next. First, she tried to look down and make out what she was coming to, but it was too dark to see anything; then she looked at the sides of the well, and noticed that they were filled with cupboards and book-shelves; here and there she saw maps and pictures hung upon pegs. She took down a jar from one of the shelves as she passed; it was labelled 'ORANGE MARMALADE', but to her great disappointment it was empty: she did not like to drop the jar for fear of killing somebody, so managed to put it into one of the cupboards as she fell past it.

Answer the following questions.

1. Alice did not think her sister's book was worth reading because there were no _____ and _____ in it.

2. What were the effects of the hot weather on Alice?

3. What deterred Alice from making her daisy-chain?

4. What seemed all unnatural to Alice at the moment it happened?
   a. a White Rabbit appearing out of nowhere
   b. the White Rabbit talking to itself
   c. the White Rabbit taking a watch out of its waistcoat-pocket

5. Parentheses are used in the second and third paragraphs to
   a. surprise the reader   b. create humour   c. add extra information

6. Underline the sentence between the second and fourth paragraphs that tells us Alice didn't think things over before she acted.

7. Was the rabbit-hole a small, shallow hole? How do you know?

8. True or False:
   a. Alice fell down a deep well after going through the rabbit-hole. _____
   b. Alice, while falling down the well, had no time to look around. _____

9. The pronoun "they" in the fourth line of the last paragraph is referring to _____ _____ _____ _____ _____.

10. Give one example to show that Alice was a thoughtful girl.

11. Fill in the blanks with the word "pass" and "past". Mind the correct tense when it is used as a verb.
   a. "_____ me the salt, please," said John.
   b. Marie _____ by the bakery on her way to school every morning.
   c. John always walks _____ me without saying anything.

12. Circle the correct answers:
   Alice's Adventures in Wonderland is considered an example of
   a. children's literature   b. fantasy   c. literary nonsense   d. nursery rhyme

Read on:

Alice's Adventures in Wonderland, commonly known as *Alice in Wonderland*, is an English novel written by Lewis Carroll in 1865. Set in a beautiful green garden, the story begins with Alice feeling bored sitting next to her elder sister who is reading. Alice then sees a rabbit running past, and following it, she falls through a deep rabbit-hole into a fantasy world of anthropomorphic creatures.

The Moonstone

Wilkie Collins

The next and last step in the investigation brought matters, as they say, to a crisis. The officer had an interview (at which I was present) with my lady. After informing her that the Diamond must have been taken by somebody in the house, he requested permission for himself and his men to search the servants' rooms and boxes on the spot. My good mistress, like the generous high-bred woman she was, refused to let us be treated like thieves. "I will never consent to make such a return as that," she said, "for all I owe to the faithful servants who are employed in my house."

Mr. Superintendent made his bow, with a look in my direction, which said plainly, "Why employ me, if you are to tie my hands in this way?" As head of the servants, I felt directly that we were bound, in justice to all parties, not to profit by our mistress's generosity. "We gratefully thank your ladyship," I said; "but we ask your permission to do what is right in this matter by giving up our keys. When Gabriel Betteredge sets the example," says I, stopping Superintendent Seegrave at the door, "the rest of the servants will follow, I promise you. There are my keys, to begin with!" My lady took me by the hand, and thanked me with the tears in her eyes. Lord! what would I not have given, at that moment, for the privilege of knocking Superintendent Seegrave down!

As I had promised for them, the other servants followed my lead, sorely against the grain, of course, but all taking the view that I took. The women were a sight to see, while the police-officers were rummaging among their things. The cook looked as if she could grill Mr. Superintendent alive on a furnace, and the other women looked as if they could eat him when he was done.

The search over, and no Diamond or sign of a Diamond being found, of course, anywhere, Superintendent Seegrave retired to my little room to consider with himself what he was to do next. He and his men had now been hours in the house, and had not advanced us one inch towards a discovery of how the Moonstone had been taken, or of whom we were to suspect as the thief.

While the police-officer was still pondering in solitude, I was sent for to see Mr. Franklin in the library. To my unutterable astonishment, just as my hand was on the door, it was suddenly opened from the inside, and out walked Rosanna Spearman!

After the library had been swept and cleaned in the morning, neither first nor second housemaid had any business in that room at any later period of the day. I stopped Rosanna Spearman, and charged her with a breach of domestic discipline on the spot.

Answer the following questions.

1. When the servants were asked to be searched, the whole investigation brought matters to a _____.

2. Who was the person most troubled by the above request? Why?

3. How do we know the writer saw his mistress most highly?

4. Who was complaining about being employed and having his hands tied??

5. Match Gabriel Betteredge with the correct descriptions:

   Betteredge was
   - a. the head of the servants.
   - b. grateful to his mistress for what she said.
   - c. to set the example for all.
   - d. reprimanded by the mistress.
   - e. grateful to the superintendent.

6. Underline the sentence in the second paragraph that infers the writer and the superintendent did not really get along.

7. What is "my lead" in the first line of the third paragraph referring to?

8. The expression "sorely against the grain" means
   a. the servants did not mind having their possessions rummaged
   b. the servants had great difficulty accepting the order
   c. the servants were not ready to eat

9. How do we know the cook and the other woman hated Mr. Superintendent?

10. Was the search successful? Underline the part of the sentence that tells us so.

11. Who was reprimanded for being in the library? Why wasn't she supposed to be there?

12. What was the person implicated in question number 11 charged with?

Read on:

The Moonstone, written by Wilkie Collins, is an early example of modern detective novels. The Moonstone, a Hindu sacred gem with a supposed curse placed upon it, has been stolen by an Englishman from India and brought back to England as a family heirloom. The stone is bequeathed to Rachel on her 18th birthday, but goes missing that very night. Everyone connected with Rachel and present at her family estate in Yorkshire is under suspicion.

Answers

Note to teachers

1. Some of the questions require students to re-examine the text for answers.
2. Some of the questions require students to think to arrive at an answer.
3. Other questions require common sense and some background knowledge. Answers to these questions are often open-ended (shown as 'multiple answers accepted').

The Dragons of Blueland

1. newspaper
2. a. funny
3. about dragons that have long been believed extinct and there were 15 of them; brave men fought their way back through treacherous sandstorms
4. a. dismissed; b. dismissal
5. he claimed he had seen a strange flying beast twice
6. a. was not an old man; b. claimed he'd seen the dragon over the city
7. a. a railway station
8. he had had anything to do with all that
9. He didn't understand Elmer's strange trip away from home.
10. He choked on a piece of toast. / He acted surprised.
11. Do Dragons Still Exist? / Fifteen Dragons Have Escaped
    (multiple answers accepted)
12. Yes—I like to read about dragons
    No—I don't like stories of fantasy
    (multiple answers accepted)

Ching Yuh and Kyain Oo: The Trials of Two Heavenly Lovers

1. in a great enclosure at the rear of the palace
2. to show their status as very important people; to be able to see better to ensure nobody was cheating
3. fold up the essay carefully and toss it over the wall into an enclosure
4. The board of examiners; His Majesty
5. were at once struck with the rare merit of the production
6. a. False; b. False; c. False
7. worshipping her son
8. he was wise and quick
9. No—he would be travelling in disguise
10. b. to execute the evil officials
11. "Pang Noo was amazed at his success"
12. to learn the whereabouts of his lady-love

Bed in Summer

1. a quatrain
2. AABB CCDD EEBB
3. a. carry the reader smoothly to the next line
4. it is still dark early in the morning in winter
5. it is still bright when he goes to bed in summer
6. The poet can see the birds still hopping on the tree and hear the grown-up people's feet.
7. a. False; b. True
8. seeing
9. He calls the people walking outside "the grown-up people."; He likes to play.
10. c. apostrophe
11. b. the poet's daily routine changes depending on the season
12. Yes—simple / short / easy to understand
    No—too short / too childish
    (multiple answers accepted)

Princess Mayblossom

1. c. butterflies' wings
2. it was so splendid that no one had ever seen anything like it before
3. c. a diamond necklace
4. she thought of nothing but Fanfaronade
5. a. synonyms
6. the fairies
7. all the gorgeous things
8. the thunder growled, and rain and hail fell in torrents / thundering, raining and hailing
9. the Queen – the royal mantle;
   the Princesses – their trains
10. croaking and mocking laughter
11. it clung so closely as if it must be nailed on
12. more than fifty pounds

Gulliver's Travels

1. escaped/survived
2. b. the storm
3. a. conjectured; b. abated; c. attempted
4. Yes—"I was in so weak a condition that I did not observe them"
5. he was extremely tired; the weather was hot; he had drunk half a pint of brandy
6. "I slept sounder than ever I remembered to have done in my life"
7. a. True; b. False
8. personification
9. his hair was fastened/tied down on each side of the ground
10. He had a bow and arrow in his hands.

11. native
12. 4 3 1 2

Rebecca of Sunnybrook Farm

1. Maplewood; the post office
2. "won't let the grass grow under her feet"
3. catch; gets
4. c. behind
5. she would be a real lady passenger or she would sit up in front with him
6. "astounded"
7. a. a simile
8. a. True; b. False
9. Her legs were dangling in the air, too short to reach the footboard.
10. smell: the big bouquet of lilacs
    see: the pink-flounced parasol
    feel: the stiffness of the starched buff calico and the hated prick of the black and yellow porcupine quills
11. it was a sweet, comfortable silence
12. c. "Welcome home!"

Wizard of Oz

1. hungry
2. No—she spread butter on it
3. a dog; it barked and wagged its tail
4. to help out her breakfast
5. a. consumed
6. a. was hanging on a peg; c. had somehow faded in colour with many washings
7. to keep insects and dirt away
8. Dorothy's old, worn shoes
9. He looked up into Dorothy's face and wagged his tail.
10. West
11. Yes—they fitted her as well as if they had been made for her
12. 1 2 3 4

The Voyages of Doctor Dolittle

1. market-place; churchyard
2. They sang strange songs as they pulled upon the ropes.
3. "by heart"
4. a. False; b. True
5. their huge brown sails
6. some gentle giants that walked amongst the houses without noise

7. "This old man was simply marvellous at making things. I never saw a man so clever with his hands."
8. a. toy ships; d. umbrellas
9. after the sun had set
10. lobsters
11. b. see too well
12. Yes—it would be fun to know what animals think
    No—I don't like animals
    (multiple answers accepted)

May Flowers

1. c. the east
2. Mayflower Club; Pilgrim Fathers
3. sewing; reading; gossiping (any two answers)
4. they had been separated all summer
5. "a chorus"
6. it's all about workingwomen, very true and very sad / Anna's mother said it might do them good to know something of the hard times other girls had
7. mature – aware of her duty;
   persistent – believed in trying
   (multiple answers accepted)
8. patting the apple blossoms she was embroidering on a blue satin
9. No—she had already had a little plan in her head and wanted to prepare a way for proposing it
10. c. wicked
11. needy people did not come her way; it all happened in books
12. "with one accord"

The Chameleon

1. in the market square;
   No—a red-haired policeman is behind him
2. "There is silence all around. Not a soul in the square . . ."
3. d. a hawker
4. hungry mouths
5. "Biting is prohibited"
6. it has been beaten
7. Yes—he seizes the dog by her hind legs
8. c. the crowd
9. an argument; Otchumyelov
10. "displaying a bleeding finger"
11. a. is a goldsmith; e. is half drunk
12. Russia

The Prince and the Pauper

1. in the prince's cabinet
2. noble knight
3. c. the lord of Norfolk; d. the lord of Surrey
4. "jewelled"
5. he had lost his mind / he could not think straight
6. lonely, uneasy, restless and distressed
7. he would be hanged
8. a. verb; b. verb
9. protection and release
10. butterflies
11. No—he was filled with nameless fears
12. 12. 1 4 2 3

The Conceited Apple Branch

1. a whole group of children
2. He had to be carried by the others.
3. laughed; kicked; rolled; plucked; kissed
4. "in childlike innocence"
5. round the neck; go across the shoulder down to the waist; about the head
6. b. unimpressive
7. a white, feathery crown
8. whoever could blow away the whole crown with one puff of breath would have new clothes before the end of the year
9. a blunt knife without a handle
10. with some, make tea for herself; with the rest, sell to the chemist for money
11. False—"There is a difference between plants, just as there is a difference between men."
12. No—the apple bough said, "That is your opinion."

Mr. Nobody

1. No—the poet is anonymous
2. funny little; quiet; a mouse
   a. a simile
3. playful/naughty behaviour to the point of being harmful to others; mischievous
4. a. False; b. True
5. d. The badges being pulled from shirts.
6. squeak; b. onomatopoeia
7. the kettles cannot boil as the fire won't start
8. cannot;
   misfortune; mistaken; misunderstand
   (multiple answers accepted)

9. to rhyme with "fade"
10. sunlight
11. Yes—I can blame him for everything that goes wrong
    No—he messes things up / he creates chaos
    (multiple answers accepted)
12. 12. Yes—it could be anybody who causes a problem

The Sword in the Stone

1. Sir Ector's castle
2. Yes—he said "excuse me"; "if you don't mind"; "sir, please, sir"; "How do you do?"
   (any two ansers)
3. formalities
4. the magician's staring at him with a kind of unwinking benevolent curiosity
5. one of the cows of Wart's guardian
6. a. He had dirty fingernails.
7. gown with stars and triangles and tarantula spectacles
8. No—the spectacles were gradually filmed and clouded over
9. if he liked peaches
10. Yes—he said, "Very much indeed." / his mouth began to water
11. 1 4 3 2
12. c. a legend

The Enchanted Castle

1. firm triumph
2. something magic
3. a crown
4. a. the urgency to be courageous
5. c. polysyndeton
6. in a small brown hand with jewelled rings on every finger
7. "extremely imposing"
8. nine: silver; red; brown; blue; green/soft green; pink; gold/rosy gold; yellow; white
9. her old-fashioned clothes
10. Marie Antoinette's ladies; history
11. "and we never knew it"
12. the enchanted princess

Little Women

1. another / one more; affection
2. to work so that the hard days need not be wasted
3. a b c d
4. sniffed
5. thought too much of her looks, and hated to work, but wouldn't anymore, if she could help it

6. do her duty instead of wanting to be somewhere else, and not be rough and wild
7. Beth – she said nothing / she was described as a quiet soul
8. Five; Mrs. March, Jo, Amy, Meg, Beth
9. a. ended a period of quiet
10. a. True; b. True (both cellar and basement are found below ground level)
11. She liked the cake and milk and did not like the cellar and the dark.
12. "who began to talk of renouncing childish things at the mature age of 12"

Black Beauty

1. a rook's wing; a. simile
2. he put his nose into his master's hand; a horse couldn't speak the human language
3. on the outside of the village; "skirted"
4. a. True; b. False
5. a large swinging window that opened into the yard
6. the first stall / a loose box
7. a low rack for hay; a low manger for corn; the horse was not tied up to do as he liked; the horse could see all that went on through the iron rails
8. b. inversion
9. He gave the horse very nice oats. He patted the horse. He spoke kindly to the horse. (any two answers)
10. a thick mane and tail; a very pretty head; a pert little nose
11. c. mistresses
12. James thinks a great deal of Merrylegs too

The Peterkin Papers

1. salt
2. He had been to college.
3. go over and ask the advice of the chemist
4. 3 1 4 2
5. finding out something that should turn everything it touched into gold
6. Yes—gold was high
7. a. the gold thimble of his aunt; d. the wedding-ring of his wife
8. "consenting"
9. No—he came near throwing his crucible at their heads
10. Agamemnon offered to pay in gold.
11. the reader
12. make a new cup and put sugar in it

Alice's Adventures in Wonderland

1. pictures; conversations
2. She felt very sleepy and stupid.
3. the trouble of getting up and picking the daisies

4. c. the White Rabbit taking a watch out of its waistcoat-pocket
5. c. add extra information
6. "In another moment down went Alice after it, never once considering how in the world she was to get out again."
7. No—it went straight on like a tunnel for some way and then suddenly down
8. a. True; b. False
9. the sides of the wall
10. She did not like to drop the empty jar labelled "Orange Marmalade" for fear of killing somebody.
11. a. Pass; b. passes; c. past
12. a. children's literature; b. fantasy; c. literary nonsense

The Moonstone

1. crisis
2. the writer's mistress; she owed to her faithful servants not to treat them like thieves
3. He called her "good", "generous" and "high-bred".
4. Mr. Superintendent / Superintendent Seegrave
5. a. the head of the servants; b. grateful to his mistress for what she said; c. to set the example for all
6. "What would I not have given, at that moment, for the privilege of knocking Superintendent Seegrave down!"
7. to give up his key
8. b. the servants had great difficulty accepting the order
9. The cook looked as if she could grill Mr. Superintendent alive on a furnace, and the other women looked as if they could eat him when he was done.
10. No—"and no Diamond or sign of a Diamond being found, of course, anywhere"
11. Rosanna Spearman; neither first nor second housemaid had any business in that room at any later period of the day
12. a breach of domestic discipline

Printed in the United States
by Baker & Taylor Publisher Services